READERS' WORKSHOP
real reading

PATRICIA HAGERTY

Scholastic Canada Ltd.

Dedicated to my own two young readers,
Brendan and Conor

Scholastic Canada Ltd.
123 Newkirk Road, Richmond Hill, Ontario, Canada L4C 3G5

Scholastic Inc.
555 Broadway, New York, NY 10012, USA

Ashton Scholastic Pty Limited
PO Box 579, Gosford, NSW 2250, Australia

Ashton Scholastic Limited
Private Bag 94407, Greenmount, Auckland, New Zealand

Scholastic Publications Ltd.
Villiers House, Clarendon Avenue, Leamington Spa, Warwickshire CV32 5PR, UK

Cover illustration by Kim Fernandes, photographed by Juanita Sarju

Canadian Cataloguing in Publication Data

Hagerty, Patricia J.
   Readers' workshop

Includes bibliographical references.
ISBN 0-590-73077-0

I. Reading (Elementary). II. Title.

LB1573.H34 1992   372.4'14   C92-093138-3

9 8 7   Printed in USA   6 7 8/9

Contents

Acknowledgements

I wish to thank the many teachers and students throughout Colorado, especially those in the Five Star School District, Adams County, for teaching me about readers' workshop.

Special thanks go to Donna Bridges, Marilyn Jerde, Teri Lehr, J.P. Roberts, Dave Paden, Kim Fox Shockley, Nancy McLean, Rob Beecher, Carol Wilcox and Lanai Wallin for their ideas and samples of children's written responses.

Thanks, too, to Laurie Jundt for reading and responding, many times, to my manuscript.

What is a readers' workshop?

Grade four

It's time to begin. Students gather on the floor in front of their teacher. What will they learn about reading today?

"Come closer, I've something exciting to share. You know, I've been wondering why and how authors choose their titles. For instance, with this book (holds up *Bunnicula,* a children's book by Deborah and James Howe), the word 'Bunnicula' is explained in the first chapter, so I understand why the author chose that title. But in this book (shows *The Other Side,* an adult book by Mary Gordon), the words of the title never appear in the book. I think the author chose that title because the main character is about to die and go 'to the other side.' In this book (*Angle of Repose,* by Wallace Stegner), the words in the title appear right near the end of the book. When I read those words I thought, 'So that's what the author meant, that's why he chose this title.'

"Thinking about titles is like solving a mystery. I wonder why some authors use words from the story in the title while others don't. Sometimes I can't figure out at all why an author used a particular title. Today when you're reading, I'd like you to think about the title of your book. How and why do you think the author chose that title? Do you find words in your story that are used in the title? If so, why do you think the author chose those words for the title? Does your book have the kind of title that makes you wonder: 'Now why did the author choose that title?' Some of you can share what you learned during the share session today — and I can't wait to see what you've found. Now, let's start our reading."

And so begins the daily readers' workshop in this fourth-grade classroom. As the students begin reading, so does Marilyn, their teacher. After a while she begins to confer with individuals or small groups of students. Some students may confer with each other. After a significant amount of reading time, the students gather again for the share session, sitting in a circle on the floor. One student begins to share her thoughts about the title of her book. Soon others clamor to share as well. Marilyn joins in when appropriate, but she doesn't direct the share session. It belongs to the students.

Grade one

Here, too, the teacher gathers her students around her. Today she's going to talk about main characters in stories.

"There's something I've noticed about authors and how they help us know who the main characters are in their stories. In *Clifford's Tricks* (she holds up the book), the author helps me figure out who the main character is in several ways. First, the main character's name is in the title. Next, I see Clifford's picture on the front cover. When I look through the book, I see him on just about every page. Those are all clues the author gives me. But you know what? The biggest clue is that the story is mainly about Clifford and all the tricks he can do. Norman Bridwell really helps me figure out who the main character is.

"Here's another book, *Just For You,* by Mercer Mayer. In this book, there's no name in the title to help me. But I've read other books like this by Mercer Mayer, and I know that these stories are about the Kritter. I see the Kritter's picture on the cover, and when I look through the book, I see his picture on every page. As I read the book I can tell that the story is mainly about the Kritter and all the things he tries to do for his mom, so I think he's the main character.

"In this book, *Two Bad Ants,* by Chris Van Allsburg, I get the feeling there are two main characters. The title talks about two ants, I see both the ants on the cover of the book, and if I turn the pages, I see that the two ants are usually together. When I read the story, I know that there are two main characters because the ants are always together and do the same things.

"Today, if you're reading a book that tells a story, see if you can figure out who the main character is and how you know. What clues did the author give you? Bring your book to the share session if you'd like to share what you've learned. Have a good time reading!"

The students in this classroom rush to their desks. Emergent readers concentrate on the pictures. Beginning readers also let the printed words help them. Teri, their teacher, spends some time reading and then begins to confer with individual students, or talk with groups of students. After about 30 minutes, the class comes together for the share session. Teri participates by talking about her own reading. She may model questions and help students make connections. She doesn't control the share, because it belongs to the students. The sharing continues until someone notices that it's time for recess. Reluctantly the students put their books back in their desks and go outside. A few decide to take their books with them.

A readers' workshop is real reading

These students and teachers are learning about reading through *readers' workshop,* a child-centered approach to teaching reading that brings the "real" world of reading into the classroom. Like all "real" readers, the students select their own reading material, read at their own pace, and talk to others about what they've read. We learn about reading by spending time reading, listening to others, and talking with others. It's the same with readers' workshop. Through self-selection, self-pacing, sharing, listening, and spending significant amounts of time reading, the children not only learn how to read, they also learn what reading is about.

This book describes the concept of readers' workshop, its principles and its components. It provides suggestions for teaching mini-lessons, conducting conferences, encouraging student responses to text, and initiating share sessions, as well as setting up a workshop and assessing student progress.

Why use a readers' workshop?

A readers' workshop takes into account the important elements of time, choice, response, community, and structure. Both Nancie Atwell (*In the Middle*) and Jane Hansen (*When Writers Read*) have described most of these elements.

Time

As in a writers' workshop, where students have large blocks of time to write, in a readers' workshop students spend a significant amount of time reading in a natural, unhurried way. They also have daily opportunities to browse and select books, and reflect on their reading. Contrast this with traditional classrooms, where students seldom read for extended periods. Instead, they spend much of their time moving around the classroom, working at centers and completing paper/pencil tasks that do little to involve them in the reading process.

Children need lots of time to be with books, interact with the author, and think about their reading.

Choice

It's important to let students select their own reading material. Here my task as teacher is twofold: I need to give my students opportunities to select from a wide variety of quality literature, but I also need to teach them how to make appropriate choices.

Students who participate in a readers' workshop invariably tell me that they like to choose their own reading material. One third-grader said to me: "When I get to choose my own books to read, I could just read all day. I hate it when we have to stop. I like to choose stories about kids like me because it makes me feel like I'm part of the story." A sixth-grader said: "When I get to choose what I want to read, I get really involved in my reading. I'm always thinking about the books I want to read next. I never liked to read much, but now I just love it."

It's clear that choice leads to ownership. Students who choose their own reading material are much more likely to be involved with and react to the text. Think of your own "real" experiences. Aren't you more involved with your reading when you've personally selected the text?

Encouraging children to choose their own reading material means that you need to have a large classroom library, stocked with many different types of quality reading materials: fiction, non-fiction, poetry, biographies, and books written by children. Ask your librarian for ideas, and look for lists in journals like *Reading Teacher* and *Language Arts*. Ask your students what books they'd like to find in your classroom collection, and check with other teachers you know.

When I say "quality," I'm speaking of books that engage students, books with rich, descriptive language, intriguing plots, and characters that stand out, books that make us sit back and say, "Oh, what a wonderful book." Quality literature has events and information we want to talk to someone else about — and quality literature is essential for an effective readers' workshop.

You and your students may have to have bake sales and car washes to get the money for the books you'll want and need — and you'll probably spend money of your own. Garage sales and secondhand book stores are good sources of reading material, and so are the central school library and public library. If your readers' workshop is working well, the students will constantly be searching for more books in and out of the classroom.

Students won't always make a "perfect" choice each time, of course. Learning how to select appropriate reading material is a process that students get better at with practice. When I talk to teachers about helping students make choices about their reading material, I usually tell the following story:

One of my friends, an excellent seamstress, told me she would help me make a dress if I'd go to the fabric store and choose a pattern and material. But when I got to the store I was completely overwhelmed. There were huge books I was supposed to look through to find a pattern I liked. Then I was supposed to find the pattern in a drawer filled with hundreds of patterns. The worst part was trying to choose the material — there were rows and rows of it! How was I supposed to know what to get? It dawned on me that there was a lot to know about choosing patterns and materials that no one had ever taught me. How could I have any sense as to what would be "appropriate"? I ended up putting the pattern on the counter and leaving the store. When my friend came over that afternoon, I told her I couldn't find anything. She threw up her hands: "I can't believe it! The whole store is full of patterns and material and you couldn't find anything?"

Do you remember students returning from the library and saying,

"I couldn't find anything"? And wasn't your reaction, "I can't believe it! The whole library is full of books and you couldn't find anything?" Because of my fabric store experience, I understand what it's like for students who have little or no experience in choosing their own reading material, and who've been given little guidance on how to do so. Learning to make appropriate choices is a process, and you have to work with students to help them learn it. One of my first mini-lessons focuses on how to select books, including how to identify books that are "easy," "just right" or "challenging" (see pages 16-17). With practice and guidance, students *will* get better at choosing what to read.

In the meantime, many teachers become discouraged about the children's choices. "Stephen King and Danielle Steele weren't what I had in mind when I started my readers' workshop," one sixth-grade teacher said to me. I think it's legitimate to put some limits on the kinds of books you want your students to read. But remember, it's up to you to bring quality literature into the classroom and draw the students' attention to it through book talks and sharing.

One teacher became concerned about a student who read the same book over and over. Have you never reread a book or part of one? Why did you do it? Because you enjoyed it? Because you didn't understand it? Because it was interesting? There are many reasons for rereading a book, and students will often reread — especially if they're just learning how to read and they've had a wonderful experience with the book. Rereading is also part of the "real" world of reading. I still have vivid memories of how I reread, over and over, the first book I read independently. Each time I got a little bit better. I'll never forget the thrill of knowing that I was now a real reader.

Students will also sometimes choose books that they never start, or that they abandon after a few pages. Here's another story I like to tell:

I have more time to read at certain times of the year than I do at others. I once went to my favorite bookstore and selected six novels, based on book reviews, advice from friends, and my own feelings about what looked interesting. I couldn't wait to get home to begin reading! Of those six, I finished four. The other two I just didn't like. Now if I, an experienced reader, could choose something I ended up not liking, couldn't students, not as practiced at choosing their books as I am, do the same? I don't really think it's a problem unless the students rarely read beyond the first few pages of any book. With those students I know I have to work extra hard to introduce good literature, and continue to teach strategies for choosing books.

It takes longer for some students to learn how to choose — and stay with — appropriate reading material. One fourth-grade teacher told me that a student in her class finally read a book from beginning to end during the sixth week of school. Until then this student would read only a few pages. The teacher continued to introduce books and offer suggestions, and her persistence paid off. This reluctant reader, who by his own admission had never finished a book, finally experienced success with self-selection. By the middle of the school year he was offering suggestions to the other students about books they might want to read.

I am often asked if students should *always* choose their own reading material. On the whole, my answer is yes. But there may be times when you want the whole class to read the same novel, especially if it's part of a particular unit of study. Or you may want to present three or four novels in a book talk and have the students select from among them, especially if all the books relate to a particular topic or author you are studying. If you want to teach a particular genre, you might gather lots of books that fit the genre and ask the students to select from those.

Response

What do you yourself do after you've read a book? You probably talk to someone about it, perhaps recommend it or lend it to someone. "Response" in a readers' workshop generally refers to students responding orally to their own reading and that of others: conferring with the teacher, talking with each other in peer conferences, or sharing in small or large groups. It may also take the form of writing, art or drama.

Community

In a readers' workshop where students actively support each other as readers, community is established. Students work cooperatively with each other, assume leadership roles when appropriate, help each other learn, encourage each other to do well, and learn to be active listeners. Everyone in the room is a teacher and a learner, and everyone's input is valued. As Mary Glover and Linda Sheppard note in their book *Not On Your Own: The Power of Learning Together,* children in classrooms with a sense of community have an appreciation of what everyone can do.

It's easy for me to tell which classrooms have a genuine sense of community and which ones don't. In one, a combination first and second grade, the teacher was amazed when I conducted a large-group share with all the students at the same time. She said that she had two share groups, one for each grade, because the second-graders got impatient with the first-graders who couldn't read.

In a first-grade classroom I sat on the floor in a circle with the students. When I asked who wanted to share first, a boy across the circle raised his hand, but before he could start, the child sitting next to me said that he couldn't read, so he shouldn't share. "Oh, he can picture share," I said. "There are many ways to share."

In both these classes the students were having trouble accepting that their classmates were reading at various levels and that these differences were okay. When students hear over and over again from their teacher that everyone reads differently because everyone isn't the same, they'll learn to be accepting of all the readers in the class, and a sense of community will emerge.

A sixth-grade class I visited did have a sense of community. I heard two students talking: "If you're having problems finding a book, I'll help you. What I do is keep a list of books I want to read. When I'm looking for a book, I take the list with me. You should try it." At the share session that day, the other students listened intently as one shared a funny part of Judy Blume's *The One in the Middle Is a Green Kangaroo.* They asked her many questions about the book, and about her reading. This class had a sense of community because students of all reading levels and abilities felt safe to share. They knew they would be supported by other readers.

I asked Lanai, their teacher, how she had helped her students achieve this sense of community. She said that at the beginning of the year the workshop didn't seem to be going well: the students were reluctant to share and had problems working with each other, and there didn't seem to be a spirit of cooperation. One day it occurred to her that she didn't know much about her students, nor did they know much about her. So she stopped the session and asked if they wanted to ask her any questions about herself. They did. They wanted to know where she was born, what her favorite food was, what she liked to do in her free time, and where she got her hair cut. One by one the students began to share about themselves as well: what they liked to eat, what they liked to read, what they liked to do in their spare time. That share session lasted two hours, and after that time, a sense of community began to develop in her classroom. Her students cared about each other as fellow students and readers. They began to share readily, accept each person's reading ability, and work together cooperatively.

As I tell my students in the pre-service classes I teach, only you, the teacher, can arrange for a sense of community to happen. A sense of community will develop if:

- you treat all readers with respect;

- you immediately stop a share session when a negative comment is made, and discuss appropriate responses;

- you share your own reading and writing with students;

- you arrange for students to work together cooperatively, and compliment them when they do;

- you believe that everyone is a teacher and a learner.

A sense of community is essential for a successful readers' workshop!

Structure

Structure refers to the organization of the workshop and the management system students can count on. A readers' workshop isn't just having students sit around and read. I don't believe that students learn to read *simply* by reading. Students learn to read because the teacher has taught and modeled strategies that good readers use, and has provided them with significant amounts of time to practice those strategies with self-selected materials. They also learn to read by responding to each others' reading, sharing their own reading and writing about their reading. Teachers significantly impact students' learning during mini-lessons, conferences and share sessions. Structure is important, and I'll discuss it more in the next section.

How to use a readers' workshop

My readers' workshops include:

- a mini-lesson;
- an activity time during which students read, confer with me or with each other, and perhaps respond to their reading through writing, art or drama;
- a share session.

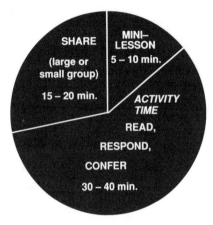

In kindergarten a whole workshop may last 30 minutes, with five minutes for a mini-lesson, 10-15 minutes for the activity time and 10 minutes for the share session. A first-grade workshop may last about 45 minutes for the first few weeks, and then move to an hour. In grade two and above I like to have at least an hour for a workshop, sometimes more in the upper grades. By all means, experiment with the structure to fit the needs of your students and the constraints of your schedule.

Mini-lessons: learning about reading

Most of my readers' workshop sessions start with a mini-lesson, when the students gather around me on the floor so I can teach them something about reading. There are some important points to remember about mini-lessons.

For one thing, I only teach what I've noticed my students need, to help them become better readers. I don't plan mini-lessons weeks in advance, but respond to what the students express about their needs as readers, in their talk and behavior. Mini-lessons need to have a genuine purpose: is the information I plan to teach going to help my students become better readers?

A fourth-grade teacher once asked me to teach his students about nouns as part of a readers' workshop, but I couldn't do it because I couldn't see a purpose for it. How does knowledge of nouns help students be better readers? I'm not saying knowing about nouns isn't important information for students at some time, but I don't think it will help them learn to read better.

They'll tell you what they need in their own way. I always carry a piece of paper with me, and as I talk to the students and listen to them read, the ideas for mini-lessons emerge. Once I noticed that a second-grader stopped at words that were names and tried to sound them out, usually in vain. He didn't realize that when he encountered a name he didn't know, he could call it anything and keep on reading. Names don't have to be pronounced correctly for comprehension to occur. I taught him that skill during the conference. Later I noticed that several of his peers had the same problem, so I added to my list of mini-lesson ideas the topic: "What to do when you come to a word you don't know, if it's a name."

Not everyone in that second-grade class will need that lesson. In any classroom at any time, a particular mini-lesson will be a review for some students and just the ticket for others, while still others may not be ready for it at all. In fact, that's not so different from an in-service session for teachers on readers' workshop. For some teachers it will be a review, reminding them of things they may have forgotten. For others it will be the impetus they need to go back to their classrooms and make a change in their reading programs. Others just aren't ready for it yet.

Mini-lessons are short: only five to 10 minutes. If they take longer, I call them "maxi-lessons." If you know in advance that your mini-lesson will more likely be a maxi-lesson, tell your students. Mine tend to groan! They love to read and don't want too many detractions during the time set aside for reading.

When teachers tell me they find it difficult to fit what they want to teach into a five to 10 minute time slot, I remind them that mini-lessons are for teaching *one* thing. Once I taught a group of kindergarten students how to find the title and author's name on a book cover. We talked about how publishers use capital and bright letters for the title and usually place it at the top of the book. We also noticed that the author's name is usually below the title, often in smaller letters. My goal wasn't to have them be able to read the title and author's name, but simply to know what those words meant on the cover of a book.

The students seemed to understand what I was teaching them, so I decided to teach them about the title page as well, and what it was for. At that point the lesson fell apart! It was just too much for them at one time. It would have been much better to wait until the next day to talk about the title page, since they already knew about the title and author. I had forgotten that mini-lessons are for teaching one thing.

For almost every mini-lesson I give, I let children's literature be the trigger — with the exception of certain procedural things. Using children's literature introduces students to books they may want to read, and makes them aware of the many complex elements of published books. The rich, descriptive language of a quality children's book helps build students' listening and speaking vocabularies. They will use phrases and words from these books in their own writing. Good literature sparks the imagination in ways we often can't see immediately. Nor do I hesitate to use my own adult books for mini-lessons. You may have noticed that Marilyn, the teacher whose workshop I described at the beginning of this book, used adult novels as well as children's literature to make her point.

Over the years I've assembled a collection of favorite books I use for mini-lessons. For example, to teach younger students how leads pull us into a book, I often use *The Terrible Thing That Happened at Our House,* by Marge Blaine. The lead, "My mother used to be a real mother," hooks the children every time.

Nancie Atwell talks about three different kinds of mini-lessons in her book *In the Middle:*

- Procedural

A procedural mini-lesson might model for students how to do a small group share, or how to give a booktalk.

- Literary

A literary mini-lesson might teach how authors develop characters in their stories, or what the setting of the story is and why it's important. The lessons I described at the beginning of this book were both examples of literary mini-lessons.

- Strategies/skills

I see a difference between a strategy mini-lesson and a skills mini-lesson. To me, a strategy is broader and more process-based — for example, what to do when you come to an unknown word, or how to make predictions to guide your reading. A skill is more focused — for example, how to use blends to figure out unknown words. When teaching skills lessons I apply the notion of *conditional knowledge* to decide what and when (and if) to teach it at all. Under what conditions will this information be useful to a reader? For instance, I don't teach the two sounds "oo" makes in a word. I find it difficult to explain to students how this will be useful to them. How many words will they encounter that have both "oo" sounds together? Not many. This skill doesn't have enough conditions to make it worth teaching.

Teachers often ask me for ideas for mini-lessons. For demonstrations of how other teachers select topics, I refer them to Nancie Atwell's *In the Middle,* Jane Hansen's *When Writers Read,* and *Read On: A Conference Approach to Reading* by David Hornsby, Deborah Sukarna and Jo-Ann Parry. At the same time, I remind them that mini-lessons come from the needs of the students, so they shouldn't use a list of mini-lessons like a checklist. The best lists are always created by teachers who take into account the level and needs of their own classrooms.

Nevertheless, here are some mini-lesson topics you might consider. I've used all of them at times; at other times I haven't needed them. Their usefulness for you will depend on the grade level you teach and the specific needs of your students.

Procedural mini-lessons

- where to sit during reading time
- giving a book talk
- how to be a good listener in a share session
- what is an appropriate noise level during reading time
- what to do when you finish a book
- what kinds of questions to ask during a share session
- running a small group share session
- self-evaluation
- getting ready for a conference
- how to have a peer conference

- where to sit during mini-lessons
- taking care of books
- keeping track of books read
- rules of the workshop

Literary mini-lessons

- differences between fiction and non-fiction books
- learning from dedications
- books that show emotion
- books written in the first, second or third person
- author studies
- how authors use quotations
- how the story setting fits the story
- characteristics of different genres
- development of characters, plot, theme, mood
- how leads hook us
- how authors use the problem/event/solution pattern
- differences between a picture book and a novel
- titles and their meanings
- characters' points of view
- examples of similes and metaphors
- examples of foreshadowing
- how authors use dialogue
- predictable and surprise endings
- use of descriptive words and phrases
- how illustrations enhance the story
- secrets in books

Strategy/skills mini-lessons

- how to choose a book
- selecting literature log topics
- connecting reading material to your own life
- tips for reading aloud
- figuring out unknown words
  - using context
  - substituting
  - using picture clues
  - using the sounds of blends, vowels, contractions, etc.

- using Post-its to mark interesting parts
- monitoring comprehension (Does this make sense and sound right?)
- asking questions while reading
- making predictions
- emergent strategies
  - concept of story
  - concept that print carries meaning
- making sense
- mapping a story
- how to retell a story orally
- looking for relationships
- looking for important ideas
- making inferences
- drawing conclusions
- summarizing a story
- distinguishing fact from opinion
- emergent reader skills: directionality, concept of "word," sound/symbol relationships

I'd like to provide here two demonstrations of mini-lessons, not for you to implement in your own classroom, but to give you a feel for what I have often experienced.

First, here is a *procedural* mini-lesson that demonstrates *how to have a small-group share session*. It might go something like this:

"For the last two weeks we've been having a large-group share during our workshop. Today let's learn how to have a small-group share. There are many ways to share in small groups, and we'll learn one way today.

"To do a small-group share you'll need to get into groups of four or five. Let's do groups of four today. You'll need to sit on the floor facing each other. Your knees don't have to touch, but it's important to face each other so you can look at each other while you share. When it's your turn to share, use a quiet voice, since there'll be lots of other small groups in the room. If you're not reading, listen carefully to the reader. One reader will start by reading a paragraph or two or a page from his or her book, or by telling about the book. If you read a page or paragraph, it should be one that you've already read to yourself.

"When you're done reading, close the book and ask, 'Are there any questions or comments?' Then the listeners get to ask you questions or make comments about the book. After the discussion is over, the reader should ask, 'Who would like to be next?' Each person in the group takes a turn. Who will volunteer to try this with me now?"

I call on three students and the four of us model the procedure. This step is imperative. Students really need to see the procedure in action before they try it. Then I invite the whole class to participate: "Today, instead of a large-group share, let's try small-group shares like the one you've just seen. Any questions? Okay, if you're ready, let's start our reading."

Notice the three important elements of this demonstration:

- I *describe the purpose* of the lesson, as clearly as I can and in terms the class is already familiar with.

- I *demonstrate the procedure,* using students if feasible.

- I *link the lesson to regular student work,* which will follow immediately after.

I usually encourage students to select their own groups — as real readers would. I think we have to give students the responsiblity of making their groups work.

A *strategy mini-lesson* I like to teach right at the beginning of the school year is *how to select reading material.* First I introduce the students to the terms "easy," "just right," and "challenging." I write the words and their definitions on a large piece of chart paper, so I can point to them as I talk.

I bring three books from my own library that for me are easy, just right and challenging. This is what I might say:

"This morning I'd like to talk to you about different levels of books. Good readers read lots of different levels of books. Sometimes they read books that are easy for them; most of the time they read books that are just right for them; and once in a while they choose books that are a challenge for them. I brought three of my books to show you what I mean.

"This book for me (I hold up a book) was an easy book. It just flowed for me. I understood all of the ideas and all of the things that were happening, and the words were easy for me to read. This book (I hold up another book) was just right for me. It was just right because I understood most of the things happening and I knew most of the words. If I didn't know a word, I tried to figure it out or skipped it. Now this book (I hold up a third book) was a challenge book for me. I had trouble understanding what was going on in it. I couldn't figure out what the characters were doing. A lot of the words were French, and that was hard for me because I don't know French. But that doesn't mean that I didn't read it. Just because a book is challenging doesn't mean that you shouldn't read it. You can learn a lot about reading by reading challenging books.

"Some readers I know only read books that are easy for them. This is a problem because it's hard to get better at reading if you only read easy books. Some readers only read challenging books. This is a problem because if you only read these books, you'll never know the joy of just flowing through a book. Remember that good readers read books at all levels.

"There's something else I want to mention, too. A book that is easy for you may be just right or a challenge for someone else. A book that's a challenge for you may be easy for someone else — it depends on how much each of you knows about the subject or topic of the book. It's okay that books that are a challenge for you might be easy or just right for someone else, because we're all different as readers.

"Today when you're reading, think about whether your book is an easy book, just right or a challenge for you, and how you know. When I confer with you we can talk about what you've learned, and some of you can share what you've learned in the share session. I can't wait to see what you've found out! Are you ready to start reading?"

A *literary mini-lesson* might touch on the difference between fiction and non-fiction books, while a *skills mini-lesson* might show students how to use blends to figure out unknown words.

With each mini-lesson, it's important to help the students connect and apply what they've learned to their own reading situations. Notice that in each demonstration I said something like, "Today when you're reading I'd like you to . . ." It's been my experience that students often don't automatically make the connections by themselves. This kind of statement helps facilitate the connecting.

Activity time: significant time to read

Activity time includes time for the students to:
- read individually and/or with a partner;
- confer with the teacher or a peer;
- respond in writing, art or drama to their reading.

Since knowing how to interact independently with print is a lifelong reading skill, I believe that teachers should ask students to read by themselves for a while before they do any partner reading. Students in primary grades love to read aloud to each other, and certainly benefit from these experiences, but I usually don't have them partner read every day. Sometimes when working with students in primary grades, I set a timer. Before the timer goes off the students read by themselves. Afterwards they can read with each other. Students in the intermediate grades usually read by themselves most of the time.

I've found that students benefit most when they select their reading material before the readers' workshop begins. I allow time during the day for them to make their selections, and encourage them to use time before or after school. If they choose their books between the mini-lesson and activity time, they're much more likely to grab any book off the shelf.

Conferring: conversations about reading

As a routine, I prefer individual conferences, but I also confer with small groups, especially when several students have read the same book or when I want to talk to a particular group of students about the same kinds of things. I usually conduct individual and small group conferences the same way.

In *The Art of Teaching Writing,* Lucy Calkins refers to conferences as the heart of a writers' workshop. I believe they're the heart of a readers' workshop too.

- They help you develop a close relationship with each student. How often do you have a chance to talk individually with each student in your class?

- They provide opportunities for stretching students, extending what they already know.

- They provide opportunties for affirming. I like to say things like: "I noticed that you skipped that word you didn't know (stopped when your reading didn't make sense, etc.) Good for you! That's something good readers do."

- They help you find out whether the students understand what they're reading. Checking for understanding means a lot more than having the students answer questions, however. Getting them to talk about their reading should be one of your main goals.

- They give you a chance to hear students read aloud, so you can examine the pattern of their miscues, information that helps you decide what strategies you need to teach.

- They help you gather ideas for mini-lessons. As I mentioned previously, I jot down ideas as I confer with the students.

When I'm conferring with students I try to use open-ended questions. Instead of asking, "Who are the main characters in the story?" I ask "What can you tell me about the characters in your story?" Not "Does your story take place in a city or the mountains?" but "What can you tell me about the setting of your story?"

Questions that focus on relating the content of the story to the student's own experiences are also helpful — for example, "Have you come across anything in your book that reminds you of something in your life?"

I often ask questions related to recent mini-lessons. For example, following a mini-lesson on the differences between fiction and non-fiction, I might ask students which kind of book they're reading and how they know. Following a mini-lesson on the different levels of books, I might ask students to tell me if they're reading easy, just right or challenging books, and how they know.

Teachers often ask me for a list of questions they can use during conferences. Books like *Toward a Reading / Writing Classroom,* by Andrea Butler and Jan Turbill, *Literature-Based Reading Programs at Work,* by Joelie Hancock and Susan Hill, and *Read On: A Conference Approach to Reading,* by David Hornsby, Deborah Sukarna and Jo-Ann Parry contain suggestions. But I urge you to compose your own questions. In my experience, teachers who have in mind the needs of their own students compose the best questions.

Remember that the purpose of questions is simply to get discussion going — you won't ask each child the same kind or number of questions. Each child has different needs, so when you ask a question, listen to the answer and take it as your lead for where to go next in the conversation. I work very hard at listening when I confer with a student; I've slowly (and painfully) learned to let the student lead the way. My goal is to talk less than the student does — not always easy, but very necessary for a successful conference.

I often start a conference by saying, "I see you're reading . . . What do you think of it?" After the student responds, I might ask, "What can you tell me about it?" I focus hard on what the student is telling me, so we can have a real conversation about the book. I always have to remember that the student may comprehend in a way I don't, since we have different backgrounds and experiences. More than one conversation with a friend about a book has shown how differently we "read" the same book. What was interesting to my friend wasn't necessarily interesting to me. Events significant for me weren't necessarily significant for him or her. It's no different in the classroom.

So how do you get a sense of what students know? I think you have to trust yourself: the more you confer, the better you'll get at talking with your students about their reading. Don't feel uneasy if you discover that a student has come away from a reading experience with less than what you feel is 100% comprehension. When you read a book for the first time, do you understand everything in it? I sure don't. Most times students won't comprehend all they read — nor should they be expected to.

Keeping in mind all these complexities, here are a number of discussion starters I've developed for myself:

- What do you think of this book?
- What's this book about?
- What were you wondering about as you read this book?
- If you had a chance to talk with this author, what would you ask him/her?
- Why do you suppose the author gave the book this title?
- Have you ever read other books by this author? If so, how are the other books like this one?
- If you could be like any character in the book, who would it be and why?
- Does this book remind you of any other books you've read? Which ones?
- If this story took place somewhere else or in a different time, how would it be different?
- Who is telling the story?
- Tell me a little bit about your favorite part.
- Can you show me a word you didn't know but were able to figure out? How did you figure it out?
- Why did you choose this book?

- Are you like anyone in this book? If so, who?
- What do you think is going to happen next? Why?
- Would you read me a favorite part?
- Is there a place in the story that you didn't understand? What did you do about it?
- Is there anyone else in the class you would recommend this book to? Who? Why?

Conferences should be short: about five minutes for individuals and 10 to 15 minutes for small groups. With practice, you'll be able to meet individually with each of your students at least once a week.

As my questions indicate, I'm not after a summary of the book, but conversation with the student (or students). I also usually ask them to read orally a part of the text they've already read silently. As they read I note which strategies they use and which they might need help with. If a teachable moment arises, I often teach the strategy right then and ask the student to try it out during his or her silent reading.

There will be times when you need to confer with students about books you haven't read. You can do this by asking generic questions to get the conference started and then taking your lead from the students. I usually tell them I haven't read the book, and ask them to tell me about it so I can decide if it's something I'd like to read. Asking them to choose only from books you've read would certainly limit their choices.

Making notes

I think it's imperative to keep anecdotal records of your conferences to use for future conferences, for meetings with parents and administrators, and for evaluation of the students' progress.

Record-keeping can take a number of forms. I'll share with you a format designed by two primary teachers I know, Teri and Dave (see next page). They use one form for each week of the school year, and record the title of the mini-lesson for each day of the week in the boxes across the top. Anecdotal records about conferences with each child are kept in the boxes beneath. They write in the children's names before they run off multiple copies.

Teri and Dave use codes to abbreviate the information they want to record. For instance:

- **ML** means that the child understood the mini-lesson; **ML̸** means he or she didn't understand.

- **FL** means read fluently; ~~FL~~ means didn't.

I use the code **C** for comprehension, and may write something like this:

- **C** = understood metaphors used in story; or **C** = didn't understand why Amelia Bedelia put the dog outside.

I also use the code **OR** for oral reading. So I might have something like this:

- **OR** = fluent; or **OR** = skips unknown words.

You can develop your own codes to capture whatever information you need.

Teri color codes each day of the week: Monday's mini-lesson is noted in red, and so are that day's conference notes; Tuesday everything's in blue; etc. That way, when she writes ML she knows what mini-lesson she's referring to. The following sample is from one of Teri's record sheets (without the color, of course):

Reader's Workshop

Week of Jan 9–13

Monday 9 Characters	Tuesday 10 Words that show More than one	Wednesday 11 Setting – when Past Present Future	Thursday 12 D.E.D journal entry	Friday 13 Beginning Middle End
1-11 "Merry Christmas M+D" - chose because it sounded interesting - confused between future and fiction Rimee ~ML~	1-9 "Hairy Bear" - comfortable with book - beginning to pick out words Bruce (ML) ☺	1-13 "Little Bear" - using beginning and ending sounds - improved FL! ☺ Molly (ML) (kind of)	1-10 "Monster at end of book" - skipped "listen" and went on Ryan (ML) E! ☺
1-11 "Christmas w/ Morris + Boris" - looked like an easy book Kristin (ML)(FL)(C)	1-12 See the Circus "I LOVE THE CIRCUS" - I know it's non-fiction I've been there Brian ~FL~ (ML)	1-10 "Jolly Postman" - still points out all words ending in s Chris ~ML~	1-9 "Boa ate the Wash" - Substitutes word that makes sense Jesse (ML)

22

Instead of individual sheets, you could use a notebook or a three-ring binder with a tab for each student. In that case you might not have to use codes because you'll have a lot more room to write. You'll also see at a glance all the notes you've kept on one student over time.

I like 2" x 4" (5 cm x 10 cm) mailing labels — they're fairly inexpensive and easy to use. Some teachers use Post-its. As I confer I jot notes on a label, and when I have time I stick the label into my notebook behind that child's tab. It's an easy way to build a running record for each child.

Peer conferences

After readers' workshops get going in your class, you'll want to teach your students how to have peer conferences. I model one with a student or another teacher, in a mini-lesson. I ask the students to spend time reading before they begin to confer with each other, and as for a group share, I write the key points on a chart for reference. We also talk about the reasons for having peer conferences:

- to share your reading;
- to get help when you're having problems understanding the author's message, the plot, etc.;
- to learn about new books to read.

Depending on the needs of your students, you may want to designate specific days and specific locations in the classroom for holding peer conferences.

One teacher I know makes up "conference cards" (about the size of this book) and prints on them the procedure for having a peer conference, as well as some conference starter questions. She places four of them along the edge of the chalkboard, and when a student wants a peer conference, he or she gets a card and finds someone to talk with. If no cards are available, the student has to wait. This system minimizes the noise level and movement in the classroom during reading time.

Responding to reading: written responses

Written responses help students make sense of their reading, reflect on their reading, and monitor their own comprehension. They also provide you with information for assessment and further instruction, and a concrete record of the children's growth and change as readers and writers.

I prefer written responses to follow quiet reading, and for fairly short times. I don't think they should be assigned every day. On the days you invite students to respond in writing, extend the workshop for 15 or 20 minutes so the students have enough time to read before they begin writing. Most teachers I've worked with ask students to use spiral-bound notebooks or sheets stapled together, which they keep in their reading folders.

Before I assign any written responses, I like to conduct a mini-lesson to teach the students how to use Post-its. I bring the novel I'm currently reading and show the students how I put a Post-it next to some interesting bit of information, something that reminds me of my own life, or perhaps a passage where I particularly like the way the author uses words. When I'm ready to write or talk to someone about my reading, I can easily locate the interesting and important places. I show them how Post-its help them "read now and write later." Students love to use Post-its. I guarantee that you won't be able to keep enough of them around.

There's no one way to incorporate written responses into the workshop. Some teachers assign specific kinds of writing, while others like the assignments to be more open-ended. I like to start a class out with fairly structured responses at the beginning of the year, but move toward less structure as soon as possible. Here are some ideas I use.

Sentence starters

Students may (but aren't required to) select one or more of the starters I give them to begin their written reaction to their reading. I like to put the starters on large charts around the room so the students can see them when they need them. Some examples might be:

- I began to think of . . .
- I love the way . . .
- I can't believe . . .
- I wonder why . . .
- I noticed . . .
- I think . . .
- If I were . . .

as I read today [handwritten annotation]

- I'm not sure . . .
- My favorite character is . . .
- I like the way the author . . .
- When I don't know a word I . . .
- I felt sad when . . .
- I wish that . . .
- This made me think of . . .

As you can see below, most students are able to use the starters quite well to react to their reading. One note of caution, however: you need to demonstrate the use of sentence starters (and all written responses!) for your students.

Abbey Teixeira
January 24, 1989
Lazy Lions, Lucky Lambs
Patricia Reilly Giff

I think Patricia Reilly Giff coze Lazy Lions, Lucky Lambs for her tiydull becos it is mrch and thay say mrch comes in like a lion and gos out like a Lamb. and thay where lazy in the begaring and lucky in the End.
if I was the athere of my Book my tiydull Would Be Richards unluk month.

Kristy
April 13, 1989
Me and the Weirdos
by Jane Sutton

I wonder why none of Cindys plans worked, I thought they were normal things to do. But now I wonder even more if Cindys going to be weird or stay at Pattis. I hope she stays with her family. Their not that weird and anyways she's lucky to have parints that whenever you do something they nevre yell at your ol ground. you. Cindy almost set the house on fire and they said it didnt matter as long as she had fun.

Double entry diaries (DEDs)

The students choose one word, phrase or sentence from their reading that makes them think of something else, and write why they chose it. The chosen word, phrase or sentence is written on the left side of the paper, and the student's response on the right.

I also model this strategy. Using a large chart. I write my response and talk to the students about the reasons for my choice. This is one of my favorite types of written responses, and I think you'll see from the examples how well the students do with it.

My sentence
I'll Fix Anthony

That sentence reminds me of when I was smaller, I wald alwase say, "I'll fix Jaime." Jame wold always say You stink. I trid to get even with her by telling my mom: Jaime said I stink. Jaime wold lagne so I just went up to my room and slamed the door as hard as I could. I'm lucky my dad wasn't home. Then I'd flop on my bed and read my ... books. I'd fall asleep after a lot of reading At dinner time

Jaime wold wake me up and ask me if I wanted dinner now or latter. That's what reminded my of my sister and me. THE END

Cassie
JAN 30, 1989
The Bears toothache
DAVID McPHAIL

DED

I tried to pull it out.

This Sitis Remid me of the time I had a los tooth. I Pulled a Little, Because I was Short Because it was My first los tooth, I Late it there, for a muthy, then I Finle Late MY mom Pull it out. She pulled it out just like that.

the
nd

"What ever happened to the brote place"
Double entry Diary

A herd of cows grazed in the east meadow Wild geese and ducks swam in the pond nearby Stretching up to a big white house was a field of soybeans making a pretty blanket of green in the spring and summer months.

This story reminded of my Grand pa farm I love it there He has cows grazing in a giant wheat field which love to drive a tractor through I like to sit up on the hill his house is in and shoot turtle he made for me On that hill I see for miles In forrow of trees and plants full of shade I pretend I'm a hunter Turtles are always around I like to go swimming in his pond It's very deep I dive of a wooden platform he made

26

The following character comparison chart is an adaptation of a DED that a second-grade teacher made. She asked her students to choose a character from their story, compare the character with someone they knew, and tell how they were alike. The example shows how one student compared her own dog with Elfie in Hans Wilheim's *I'll Always Love You*.

Name: April		Title: I'll Always Love You
Character Comparison		
Character	Someone I Know	How are they alike?
Elfie	My dog	My dog got in alot of mischief just like Elfie. When we let my dog in she almost ate the cat up. My dog even jumped up on the dinner table. My dog got in trouble for eating my brothers steak and pork chop. She got in trouble for going poop on the floor. She ran off in the feild and got in trouble for that alot of times. There's only one thig she didn't get in trouble for and that's getting hit by a car.

Story frames

Story frames are helpful for teaching students how to summarize a story, describe the setting, analyze a character, or compare characters. (See Gerald Fowler in the November 1982 issue of *Reading Teacher*.) Story frames contain words and phrases linked together by blank spaces. After reading their books, the students fill in the spaces with their own words. Even first-graders can complete story frames if you model them first.

JOEY

STORY FRAME WITH ONE CHARACTER

Our story is about __toad and Frog__
__go to fly a kite__

__toad__ is an important character in our story.
tried to __get the kite in__
__the air__

The story ends when __they finlly__
__got the kit in the__
__air.__

(probably
probly)

Kristy   Important idea or Plot
1-31-89
Miss Pickerell on the Moon
by Ellen MacGregor and Dora Pentell

In this story the problem starts when
Miss Pickerell's cow gets sick. After that,
Mr. Esficott gives the cow a cat
for a birthday present. Next, Pumpkin
the cat gets sick. Then Miss Pickerell
heres about mold growing on the
moon that might help the virus.
The problem will probably be slord
when they get the samples and
they will give it to the animals and
in a few weeks they'll be as good
as new

{Charlottes Web}

Aaron

Character analysis

__Willbur__ is an important character in
my story. __Willbur__ is important because __he__
__is very special to every-__
__one.__

Once, he __tride to spine a spider__
__web.__

Another time, __he jumped out of his__
__fence__

I think that __Willbur__
            (character's name)

is __sensitiv__
      (character's trait)

because __when someone is meen__
__to him he starts crying__

Character Comparison

Gina
1-31-89
Matthew Looney's Invassion of the
Earth
by Jerome Beatty JR.

Matthew Looney and Hector Hornblower
are two characters in my story. Hector
Hornblower is terrible while Matthew
Looney is being just great. For instance
Hector Hornblower tries to get in a
lot of trouble and Matthew Looney
tries to keep him out of trouble.
Hector Hornblower learns a lesson
when Matthew Looney gets to go
and look for all the earthlings.

Report cards

Terry Johnson and Daphne Louis's book *Literacy through Literature* contains a wealth of ideas for written responses. One of these is the report card. Students choose a character from their story and grade him or her on different subjects. They also must say why that particular grade is being given. The example this fourth-grader completed tells a lot about her understanding of the book.

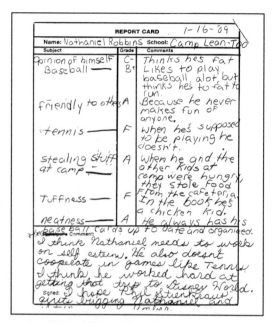

REPORT CARD	1-16-89	
Name: Nathaniel Robbins	School: Camp Lean-Too	
Subject	Grade	Comments
opinion of himself	C-	Thinks hes fat
Baseball ———	B+	Likes to play baseball alot, but thinks hes to fat to fun.
friendly to others	A	Because he never makes fun of anyone.
tennis ———	F	When he's supposed to be playing he doesn't.
stealing stuff at camp ———	A	When he and the other kids at camp were hungry, they stole food from the cafeteria.
Tuffness ———	F	In the book he's a chicken kid.
neatness ———	A	He always has his baseball cards up to date and organized.

Teachers Comment:
I think Nathaniel needs to work on self esteem. He also doesn't coopelate in games like Tennis I think he worked hard at getting that trip to Disney World.
Signed: I hope Phil Stientraus quits bugging Nathaniel and

Dialogue letters

Nancie Atwell describes her use of dialogue letters with her middle-school students: they write to her about their reading and she writes back. Younger students usually write one letter after they've read an entire book, while older students may write several letters about a book while they're reading it. Your job is to write back to them, commenting on what they've written and adding your own thoughts.

Dear Mrs. Hagon
I read a book call JUMANJI. It's about a boy and a girl Who get relly bord. So they go to the park. And the boy finds a game calld Jumanji And they take it home. And every time one of them roll the dice somthing hapens. I liked the part when the lion got his head stuck under the bed because it made me laf.
Love,
Aaron

Dear Aaron,

Jumanji is an interesting book, isn't it? I love the way it ends because it makes you think, "Now, what's going to happen to those two boys who just found the game? Will the game become "real" like it did in the first part of the book?
I think Chris Van Allsburg has a great imagination, don't you?

Love,
Mrs. H.

Handwritten journal entries between Matt and Ms. Fox:

5-8-89

Dear Ms. Fox,
The book I'm reading now is called Maybe a mole. I haven't got very far on it. I'm only on page 8. One thing I learned so far that moles are nearly blind. But the mole I'm reading about isn't blind. His family kicked him out because he could see, and they couldn't. Maybe they are jealous. I can't imagine living in a hole with moles and not being able to see.
Love,
Matt 5/8/89

Dear Matt
I'm really glad you are reading that book. I really like it a lot — the whole idea is neat to me. I think the author came up with the idea by saying to himself "What if there was a mole who could see?" How is your chunk reading coming along? Is it working for you? Is it fast? Does it let you understand your book?
Love,
Ms. Fox

5-15-89

Dear Ms. Fox,
My goal is coming well. My goal is read faster and understand what I read. Its coming great for me. When I first made my goal. I was read a little book. I had just started it. The next day I went to school, I read like 5 or 6 chs of the book I understanded it so much I could take a test on it. I finished that book in a jippy. I hope I keep that way.
Love,
Matt

Open-ended responses

One fourth-grade teacher I know asks her students to write open-ended responses in their literature logs at least twice a week, leaving it to them to decide when to respond and what to write about. She spends a lot of time modeling by sharing her own written responses in the log she keeps herself. The students' responses vary: passages they find to be particularly interesting or well written, story events that remind them of things that happen in their own lives, words or phrases that move them, sometimes their discoveries about themselves as readers. In the section on share sessions you'll find two examples of this kind of journal entry.

Responding to reading: other responses

You might invite your students to map out stories, make webs, write letters to authors, write known and unknown words found in the story, write words from the story that contain certain sounds, or just write about anything that seems important to them. I often have younger readers fold a paper into three parts and write what happened at the beginning, middle and end of the story. Once you get going with a readers' workshop, many creative ideas of your own will emerge.

Students can also respond to their reading through art, drama and music. Making a diorama in a shoebox, drawing a picture, making a book jacket or poster advertising the book — these are all productive ways in which students can respond to their reading. So, too, are putting on a skit or play, or acting out a favorite scene. *Ideas and Insights: Language Arts in the Elementary School,* edited by Dorothy Watson, contains numerous ideas you'll find useful.

Just as written responses should not take more time than the actual reading, neither should other types of responses. Some of these activities can be completed at home or in the students' free time at school. Especially when you ask your students to complete a particular project relating to a book, you may need to provide a block of time for them to work on it.

Share sessions: talking about books

Each daily workshop ends with a share session that gives the students an opportunity to find out about themselves and each other as readers and writers, as well as providing a framework for constructing meaning through active involvement with other learners.

Teachers keep asking me whether share sessions are important, and I keep telling them that they are *essential,* for themselves as well as for the students. Here's some evidence from two fourth-grade students' literature logs:

Cheyann Churchill
4/30/90

I think being able to share is like somebody giving you a big waffle ice cream cone with 3 scoops of strawberry ice cream. It is as much of a treat to get a ice cream cone as it is to share my reading. It makes me feel real important when I can share what I have to say about my reading. When you get the chance to share you can express your feelings, and it helps me understand my book better. I like it when people ask me questions because it gets me to think.

March 2

Dear Journal,

The other day I was reading my book _Dollhouse Murders_. I came to a really exciting part and I couldn't believe it. I could hardly wait until share time, so I could tell somebody about my book. You know what... everyone really listened, and now I can't believe how many people are reading my book. It makes me feel great because I'm the one who told everyone about this book. Jessica is always the one to give me ideas about good books, and now I gave her one.

Stephanie Baker

These students know that share sessions:

- validate their ideas;
- give them an opportunity to express what they've learned;
- encourage positive feedback from others;
- provide them with an avenue for connecting their prior knowledge and experience with the text;
- give them an opportunity to go beyond the literal retell level to a more in-depth analysis and emotional interpretation of reading;
- help strengthen their skills as listeners, questioners, and decision-makers.

Share sessions are important for teachers too. They:

- provide you with a systematic way to observe and evaluate student interaction;
- give you an authentic setting for assessment;
- help you become aware of strategies individual students use as readers;
- provide for the integration of all components of literacy development (reading, writing, listening, speaking, and thinking);
- help strengthen a sense of community.

For my early share sessions in a classroom I usually call together the whole group. We all sit in a circle on the floor, in such a way that we can all see each other and it's easy to make eye contact with those who are talking. Sometimes the floor is open to anyone. At other times I ask specific students to share — for instance, when I've just conferred with a student who had something especially interesting to say.

Rarely do students tell me they don't want to share. In fact, in the lower grades everyone usually wants to share every day, which isn't always possible. One way I avoid confusion and frustration is by making a set of small cards numbered from 1 to 5. As I confer with students, or just walk around the room, I give out the numbers. Those students are the ones who are guaranteed an opportunity to share that day.

After a week or two of community shares, I teach the students how to have a small-group share. These groups may be as small as three students or as large as ten, depending on the purpose of the share. There are many reasons to have students share in small groups. Sometimes several students may be studying the same book, or reading and studying books in the same genre. A group of students may be reading biographies about the same person, written by different authors. Sometimes students share in small groups with others who are reading books by the same authors. Small-group shares can also be encouraged for students who are reading unrelated books. This kind of share was demonstrated earlier. Students can also be paired for sharing. The reasons for small-group sharing are equally valid for paired shares.

What do students talk about during share sessions?

Often students share what they learned from a mini-lesson and the book(s) they read after it. You might start this kind of share by asking, "So, what did you find out?" Or you might start by asking some of the students to give book talks to try to convince the others to read the books they enjoyed. You might go around the circle and ask students to capture their book in one sentence, or ask them to read from their literature logs.

I often ask students to read aloud in both large and small groups. The procedure is the same whether the group is large or small. Four or five students read a paragraph from their books and the rest of us get to ask questions or make comments about the book. Large-group shares provide good opportunities for students to talk about the goals they have as readers, or to spend time evaluating what is going well with the workshop or what they would like to change.

Lucy Calkins mentions "secret questions" in a chapter in *The Art of Teaching Writing*. These are usually used with small groups. Each group gets a question as the share begins — for instance, "What's the setting of your book and why is it important to the understanding of the story?" or "How is the main character of your story like or not like you?" When I use secret questions, I write them on cards and give one card to each group. Sometimes each group gets the same question; sometimes they get different questions.

Many teachers ask me what their role is during share sessions. In large-group shares, you are a learner and a teacher, just like everyone else. The share doesn't belong to you; it belongs to the students. Your job is to participate when appropriate — for instance, to share what you've learned from your own reading. There are usually times during a share when you can help the students make connections or apply specific knowledge to their reading. When I first have large-group shares, I tend to be more directive, but only to demonstrate the kinds of questions I would like students to ask. I also want to model for them how to keep the conversation going. My goal, however, is to turn the share sessions over to them as soon as possible. I want them to have a dialogue with each other about their books.

When using small-group shares, your role is to move from group to group, joining in where appropriate and helping the students make connections with their own reading. A teacher once told me that during the small-group shares in her class the students would talk about other things besides their reading — just the way adults sometimes do! We don't always stick to the topic either. Your students might wander at times, and if you feel it's really a problem, write down on your list of mini-lessons that you need to work more on the standards for small-group shares. Remember, the more your students participate in small-group shares, the better they'll get at it.

Assessment

Many teachers are still required to assess and report in ways that clash with their own beliefs about learning and teaching. And teachers who use readers' workshops often ask me: "How do I grade?" They realize that what goes on in a readers' workshop doesn't easily translate into marks on traditional report cards. "How do I explain to parents how I arrived at a grade?" is a critical question to these teachers.

When I think of assessment in this context, I think of the time when I was pregnant with my first child. Early in my pregnancy I focused on other pregnant women, but in the last stages I began to look for women who had recently given birth. My thoughts were, "She did it and she's walking," or "See, she gave birth and she seems normal. You can do it, Pat!" Since I had never given birth before, I had no idea how to go about doing it (despite Lamaze classes), and I really wondered if I would be able to do it and live to tell the tale. I tried to convince myself that millions before me had given birth, so I could do it too.

For assessment and reporting, do what I did in my pregnancy. Look for and talk to others who have done it, and you'll begin to think, "Yes, I can do it too." Hundreds of teachers before you have also wondered, "How will I grade my students using this format for teaching reading?"

There is no one way to assess student progress in a readers' workshop. I'll provide some ideas in this section, but I'm sure you'll find your own way once you get going with the workshop. In fact, if you're in a school where a number of teachers are using a workshop, or want to use one, and your report cards are fairly traditional, I predict that you'll soon be talking together about changing the report cards to reflect how you teach reading.

Nancie Atwell suggests that a grade be based on three parts:

- how the student followed workshop procedures;
- the quality of the student's written responses;
- the student's progress toward goals that have been set collaboratively by the student and the teacher.

How will you know if the student has followed *workshop procedures*? You'll know because you've had regular conferences with that student: you've become a "kid watcher" and kept anecdotal records. You're very much aware of who settles down with a book when the workshop begins, who pays attention during the mini-lesson, and who participates in the share session.

When evaluating students' *written responses,* consider how the students are doing based on their individual ability, not on how the rest of the class is doing. Students are all very different in their ability to get thoughts down on paper. Ask yourself if they're doing as well as they can, and go from there.

At the beginning of each grading period, the students should have *goals* to work toward. You can teach a mini-lesson on goal-setting, and then ask each student to choose one and write it down. When you next confer with each student, add one goal that you would like for that student. Then, sit down together at the end of the grading period and look at the progress toward these goals. Completion of both goals rates an "A" (or whatever your highest grade is) for one-third of the grade. Completion of one goal and progress toward the second might be a "B." Progress toward both goals might rate a "C." Below are lists of goals developed by students in a second/third-grade combination class and a fourth-grade class.

GOALS (1–3)	GOALS (3–6)
try and read at least one book at home each night	skip an unknown word and come back to it
learn new words	substitute a word
keep track of books read	keep my eyes on my book
share at least one good book a week	choose more "just right" books
read new kinds of books	do more chunk reading
read longer books	ask myself, "does this make sense?"
read chapter books	read at home every night
read more by myself	stick with a book
skip unknown words	read "fatter" books
tell the story outloud to someone	read more books by _____
read favorite books again	write better responses
recommend books to other kids	participate in share sessions
	skim or skip uninteresting parts

A checklist of qualities you consider important might also help you assess. Toward the end of the grading period, check off whether the student has demonstrated each quality consistently (+), shown it some of the time (✓), or is working on it (/). This information can be combined with information from anecdotal records and the student's reading folder to arrive at a grade.

What are the qualities included on such a checklist? The best ones are those you arrive at yourself. What do you think is important for your students to know about reading? You might consider the following:

- shows enthusiasm for reading;
- initiates own reading;
- chooses appropriate books;
- uses appropriate strategies to develop meaning;
- actively participates in share sessions;
- writes effective journal responses;
- follows the rules of the workshop;
- is attentive during mini-lessons;
- sustains reading for at least . . . minutes;
- reads a variety of genres;
- uses prediction before and during reading;
- uses a skip-it strategy when encountering unknown words;
- reads fluently;
- keeps a log of books read;
- makes thoughtful, varied responses to reading;
- uses silent reading time appropriately;
- engages in self-evaluation;
- requests meaningful help in reading.

When you think of these characteristics in connection with specific students in a readers' workshop, you'll easily know whether those students demonstrate the characteristic consistently, show it some of the time, or are working on it, because you are a "kid watcher." You know what the children are doing because you've observed them, talked with them, and kept anecdotal records on them.

You might consider making copies of the checklist and sending them home with the report cards. You'll find that parents will appreciate knowing this kind of information about their children as readers. They'll learn much more about their children's progress from a checklist than a single letter-grade can convey.

One fourth-grade teacher faced a problem. The report card she had to use required her to name the grade level at which her students were reading. When she used a basal, the answer was easy. But now she was using a readers' workshop, and the books her students selected didn't always indicate grade levels. She told me she wasn't sure what grade level her students were reading at, and asked what she could say to parents about this.

As we started to talk, it became clear that she did know the approximate reading level of each child. I asked her if she could group her students into three groups: "higher," "middle" and "lower" readers. She could do that easily. When I asked her what grade level she thought the "middle" readers were at, she answered "fourth." So the "higher" must be fifth and sixth, and the "lower" must be third. One child (she thought) was reading at a level below that. Using this information, she was able to tell the approximate grade level each of her students was reading at, and share this information with their parents.

Self-assessment is an important component in readers' workshop as well. It can take many forms. I've already mentioned how students set goals for themselves and talk with you about progress toward those goals before you give them grades. They can also respond to questions such as those Jane Hansen talks about:

- What is something new you've learned to do in reading?
- What would you like to do well in reading?
- What would you like to learn so you can become a better reader, and how will you go about learning that?

It's also interesting to ask students to respond to the same checklist you are using, or a similar one. *Read On: A Conference Approach to Reading* has an excellent student self-evaluation form you might find useful.

Before you give a student a grade, you both sit down, go over the checklists, and decide on what that grade should be. One fourth-grade teacher I know asked her students to give themselves a grade in reading and tell why they decided on that particular grade. Of the 27 students in her class, 25 gave themselves the same grade she was going to give. The other two gave a lower grade. Students are very aware of how they're doing. At all grade levels, both teacher and student should have input into the grade.

When you use readers' workshop, you may give a lower-level reader a high grade in reading, but this doesn't mean the student is reading at grade level, or better than others in the class. Let's say the lowest reader in your class follows workshop procedures, writes responses to the best of his or her ability in a response journal, and achieves one goal and makes progress on the other. Would you give this student a "D" because he or she is not yet able to read some of the more challenging books as readily as the others do? I hope not. But however you decide to grade, it's important that you explain to parents both the grade and the reason for giving it.

I want to make one more point about assessment of student progress. All grades contain some measure of subjectivity, even in the most rigid grading systems. No two teachers grade the same because we all see students in a different way. How you grade your students in reading this year may change next year. It's crucial that you're aware of your criteria, and that you have reasons for them. Then relax. Take it from me, and from all those who've gone before you: you *will* find a grading system that works for you!

Getting started

I hope I've given you enough information about the readers' workshop approach that you'll seriously consider adopting it for your own classroom. What do you need to do to get ready?

First, you need to create a literate environment in your classroom. Here are some suggestions:

- Put up posters. Many publishers of children's books and book clubs provide them, as do organizations like the Children's Book Centre in Canada and the American Library Association in the United States.

- Set up a reading corner with pillows and/or beanbag chairs where students can go to read quietly.

- Create a large space in the room for students to gather for mini-lessons and large-group shares.

- One teacher I know has a "literary bulletin board" where she puts articles and notes of interest about reading. Publishers of children's books provide lots of information about authors. Watch your local paper for book reviews and articles that would be of interest to your students, and ask them to watch for things they'd like to add.

- Give book talks. A large classroom library means nothing if the students don't know what's in it. Start talking about the books in your classroom, and ask your school librarian to give book talks to your students when they visit the school library. When I give a book talk, I usually say something about the author and I read what's on the back cover. I may even read aloud a whole chapter to get the students "hooked" into wanting to read the book.

- Share your own reading (and writing). Remember what I said about classrooms having a "sense of community" in order for a readers' workshop to be truly successful. Sharing your own reading and writing with students helps develop that sense of community and shows them how much you value reading and writing yourself.

- Collect books for your classroom library. I suggest that you start by talking to your school administrator about buying literature books instead of basals and workbooks. (For making your case, see *Reading Teacher,* October, 1989, which discusses the enormous cost of materials for seatwork.)

I mentioned previously that you may have to spend some of your own money at garage sales, secondhand stores and flea markets. Asking parents to donate books to your classroom library is another good way to build your supply, as is ordering from book clubs. You can borrow books from the local public library, as well as from your own school library. If you have basals in your classroom, be sure to include them; some students will find stories in them that they enjoy reading. Then there are the bake sales and car washes teachers and students organize to earn money for books. It's a sad commentary that the very people who are in charge of creating a literate society (teachers) are seldom given the funds to do so.

Once you have lots of books, place them in inexpensive plastic baskets and spread them all around the room, instead of keeping them in just one location. Decide with your students how the books should be grouped: by author's last name, by genre, by type of book, etc. In kindergarten and first-grade classrooms, I like to set the baskets on the tables the students sit at. Children at this level often go through numerous books during a single reading period, and that way the books are easy for them to get to — and movement in the classroom is minimized. Rotate the baskets each time you have a workshop.

Before you get started, you'll need to set up student folders. They will contain: a notebook (literature log or response log) for written responses, the list of goals you and the students have decided on, a record of the books read and, for older students, a list of books they want to read. I prefer folders with pockets. When keeping track of books read, I ask older students to record the name of the book, the author, the date started and the date finished. You might also ask them to rate the book in some way (five stars is absolutely wonderful, one star is not so good). If it takes students longer to write the name of the book than it does to read it, as I find it often does with younger students, I provide a page of circles. Every time they read a book, they color in a circle to help keep track of the number of books they've read.

You'll also need to set up your own notebook (I prefer a three-ring binder) for keeping forms for anecdotal records. Depending on the way you decide to keep your anecdotal records, you may also need several pages with the students' names listed down the left. One of these pages can be for shares and one for conferences. I use checks to keep track of who is and who isn't participating, in both conferring and sharing.

To help you keep track of the mini-lessons you've given, you might make a calendar for each month of the school year. However, if you use the system I described earlier (see pages 21-23), you won't need a calendar. Don't forget to keep a page in your notebook for mini-lessons you still want to give.

To complete the notebook, you'll need a copy of the goals you and the students have decided on. I keep each student's goals on a sheet of paper next to the anecdotal records for that student.

Finally, you and the students will need to set the standards for the workshop. You can do this in one of the first mini-lessons you give. What rules and procedures should the students follow? I like to write these on a large sheet of chart paper that stays up in the room. Nancie Atwell suggests a number of standards. Some of these include:

- You must read for the entire time.
- You can't do homework — you must read a book.
- You may not disturb others.
- You may sit anywhere.

Some others I've used include:

- Listen when asked.
- Be ready to share when asked.
- Choose books before the workshop begins.

There's no one set of standards that's good for all students. Take your lead from them. In one classroom I noticed that some children were having problems concentrating because of a constant flow of students to and from the bathroom. At the beginning of the share session I mentioned what I had noticed, and asked what they thought we might do about it. They were the ones who suggested that we add "no trips to the bathroom" to our list of standards.

And in conclusion . . .

Now that you've read about readers' workshops, I hope you'll give them a try. I, and the many teachers I've worked with, can testify that one of the biggest benefits of teaching reading this way is that the students love to read. Not only can they read and use strategies important to good reading, but they *ask* to read. When you look around your room during a quiet reading time and see your students deeply engrossed in books, you'll know you've given them a lifelong gift.

And you'll discover many personal benefits from teaching reading through readers' workshops. You'll be able to base your teaching decisions on your observations of what the students need. You'll be a professional in control of your own reading program. You'll be a teacher and a learner too; your students will help you learn as you help them learn. You'll know you're helping them become the best readers they can be.

The "real world" of reading is possible for all of us, students and teachers both. I hope you'll bring this world into your own classroom.

References

Professional books

Atwell, Nancie. *In the Middle.* Portsmouth, NH: Heinemann, 1987.

Butler, Andrea and Jan Turbill. *Towards a Reading/Writing Classroom.* Portsmouth, NH: Heinemann, 1984.

Calkins, Lucy. *The Art of Teaching Writing.* Portsmouth, NH: Heinemann, 1986.

Fowler, Gerald. "Developing Comprehension Skills in Primary Students Through the Use of Story Frames," in *Reading Teacher,* vol. 36, no. 2, pp. 176-179, 1982.

Glover, Mary and Linda Sheppard. *Not On Your Own: The Power of Learning Together.* Richmond Hill, ON: Scholastic, 1990.

Hancock, Joelie and Susan Hill. *Literature-Based Reading Programs at Work.* Portsmouth, NH: Heinemann, 1988.

Hansen, Jane. *When Writers Read.* Portsmouth, NH: Heinemann, 1987.

Hornsby, David, Deborah Sukarna and Jo-Ann Parry. *Read On: A Conference Approach to Reading.* Portsmouth, NH: Heinemann, 1988.

Jachym, Nora, Richard Allington and Kathleen A. Broikou. "Estimating the Cost of Seatwork," in *Reading Teacher,* vol. 43, no. 1, pp. 30-37, 1989.

Johnson, Terry and Daphne Louis. *Literacy through Literature.* Richmond Hill, ON: Scholastic, 1988. Available in the U.S. from Heinemann.

Watson, Dorothy, ed. *Ideas and Insights: Language Arts in the Elementary School.* Urbana, IL: NCTE, 1987.

Other books

Blaine, Marge. *The Terrible Thing That Happened at Our House.* New York, NY: Scholastic, 1975.

Blume, Judy. *The One in the Middle Is a Green Kangaroo.* New York: Dell, 1981.

Bridwell, Norman. *Clifford's Tricks.* New York: Scholastic, 1969.

Gordon, Mary. *The Other Side.* New York: Viking, 1989.

Howe, Deborah and James. *Bunnicula.* New York: Avon, 1979.

Mayer, Mercer. *Just For You.* New York: Western Publishing, 1975.

Stegner, Wallace. *Angle of Repose.* New York: Doubleday, 1971.

Van Allsburg, Chris. *Two Bad Ants.* Boston: Houghton Mifflin, 1988.

Wilheim, Hans. *I'll Always Love You.* New York: Crown Publishing, 1985.